Canals Are Water Roads

Canals Are Water Roads

a building block book

Lee Sullivan Hill

Carolrhoda Books, Inc./Minneapolis

For Adam, with love
           —Mom

For metric conversion, when you know the number of miles, multiply by 1.61 to find the number of kilometers.

The photographs in this book are reproduced through the courtesy of: Erwin C. "Bud" Nielsen, "Images International," front & back cover, pp. 9, 11, 17, 28; James P. Rowan, pp. 1, 7, 13; Jerry Hennen, pp. 2, 5; © Diane C. Lyell, pp. 6, 23, 26; © Nik Wheeler, pp. 8, 19, 29; © Howard Ande, p. 10; © Betty Crowell, p. 12; Joseph F. Viesti/Viesti Associates, Inc., pp. 14, 15, 24, 27; © Cheryl Koenig Morgan, p. 16; Jack Olson, p. 18; © William H. Johnson, p. 20; Bureau of Reclamation, p. 21; World Bank, p. 22; New York State Thruway Authority, p. 25.

Carolrhoda Books, Inc. c/o The Lerner Publishing Group
241 First Avenue North, Minneapolis, MN 55401 U.S.A.

Library of Congress Cataloging-in-Publication Data

Hill, Lee Sullivan, 1958–
    Canals are water roads / by Lee Sullivan Hill.
       p.   cm. — (A Building block book)
    Includes index.
    Summary: Describes different canals and explains their usefulness.
    ISBN 1-57505-024-2
    1. Canals — Juvenile literature. [1. Canals.] I. Title. II. Series: Hill, Lee Sullivan,
1958– Building block book.
TC745.H55 1997
386'.4—dc20   96-22097

Manufactured in the United States of America
1 2 3 4 5 6 SP 02 01 00 99 98 97

Canals connect water. They cross land like water roads.

Did you ever cut across a neighbor's yard? Ships take a shortcut across Panama. The Panama Canal cuts almost 8,000 miles off a trip between the Atlantic and Pacific Oceans.

The Panama Canal opened in 1914. Some canals are much older. This canal in Amsterdam is hundreds of years old. Ride a barge down the canal. Don't forget to duck for the low bridges!

Some canals are long. The Grand Canal meanders more than a thousand miles, from southern China to Beijing.

Others are short.
This canal carries water.
There are really two
kinds of canals. One, like
this farmer's canal, carries
water to dry places. It is
called an irrigation canal.

The other kind of canal carries boats and barges. Tons of cargo travel on the Chicago Sanitary and Ship Canal.

Imagine a world where everyone traveled by boat. If you lived in Venice, you would use canals every day. Would you ride a motorboat to school?

In Colonial times, Americans built canals
where rivers didn't run. Roads were just dirt
tracks. Canal boats were faster than wagons.
George Washington was one of the planners
of the Chesapeake and Ohio Canal.

You can still travel on some old canals.

Mules and horses walk along the towpath.

They pull low-slung boats through the water.

As America grew, more canals were built. Immigrants dug miles of ditches for the Erie Canal. When it opened in 1825, people rushed to see the wonder. Could boats really climb hills and mountains?

You can see for yourself. Locks lift boats up and down the hills. They act like huge water steps. Locks on the Erie Canal help people cross mountains.

How do locks work? Think about your bathtub or wading pool. When you pull the plug, a toy boat lowers as the water drains away.

Put back the plug. Turn on the water. As the pool fills, the toy floats higher. (Oops, don't forget to turn off the water!)

Water power lifts boats and barges up and lowers them down, just like toys in the tub.

There are five locks between Lake Superior
and Lake Huron. Between the two lakes, water
runs fast and hard. Ships go through locks so
they don't have to go over the falls. But these
locks don't work in winter. Why not?

Water freezes. Ship traffic stops. Skating time. Wouldn't it be fun to skate for miles up and down a canal? When your feet get tired, it's hot chocolate time!

Salt water in the Cape Cod Canal never
freezes. Ships travel between Boston and
New York all year long.

Water in hot places never freezes, either. Farmers in hot, dry places bring in water for irrigation. Maybe the Brussels sprouts your mother made you eat last night grew right here in the desert.

All canals need maintenance to keep working smoothly. Farmers clean out irrigation canals with their shovels.

Workers use dredges to clean big canals.
Dirt builds up, layer upon layer, on the bottom
of a canal. Dredges scoop it out. Without
dredges, ships would get stuck in the muck.

Next time you fill the bathtub, watch water power lift your toys.

Think about canals when you slip down a water slide or when you eat your vegetables.

When you grow up, you could work
on a canal.

You could sail a ship on the Panama Canal.

You could travel through locks down the Erie. You could even be a farmer and grow Brussels sprouts in the desert.

Canals are needed now as much as ever in the past. They turn desert into farmland. They lift barges over mountains.

Canals bring people and places closer together.

A Photo Index to the Canals in This Book

Cover A taxi-boat speeds along a canal in Venice, Italy. Would you like to go for a ride?

Page 1 A motor launch goes down the Prinsengracht Canal in Amsterdam. The canal was built in the 1600s. In the 1940s, Anne Frank lived in the Annex behind Prinsengracht 263.

Page 2 The sky above the Soo Locks in Sault Sainte Marie glows in early evening. Ships travel from Lake Superior to Lake Huron on the Saint Marys River. The locks carry ships safely around the rapids and falls. Along one shore is Ontario, Canada, and on the other is Michigan, USA.

Page 5 A fishing boat motors down the Sturgeon Bay Canal in Door County, Wisconsin. The canal, finished in the late 1800s, opened a shortcut between Green Bay and Lake Michigan.

Page 6 The Panama Canal was started in 1881, but many workers died of malaria. Work slowed and money ran out. Then in 1904, President Teddy Roosevelt got involved. He sent Dr. William Gorgas to Panama along with engineers. Ten years later, in 1914, the first ship passed through the Panama Canal.

Page 7 More than 1,000 bridges cross the canals of Amsterdam in the Netherlands. Canals are part of everyday life. In Amsterdam, you can even rent a houseboat or sleep in a floating hotel.

Page 8 Some parts of the Grand Canal are no longer in use, but it's still busy here in Suzhou, China. It looks like rush hour.

Page 9 A canal branches off into a small feeder irrigation ditch. It's watering crops near Florence, Arizona.

Page 10 Canals and rivers cut across Illinois. They connect Chicago and Lake Michigan to the Mississippi River. This barge is traveling north to Chicago on the Chicago Sanitary and Ship Canal system.

 **Page 11** The Grand Canal in Venice, Italy, runs through the center of the city. Smaller canals (nearly 200 of them) carry gondolas and motorboats around the rest of Venice.

 **Page 12** President George Washington knew that canals would help open up America's frontier. That's why he helped plan what became the Chesapeake and Ohio Canal. The canal was to connect the Potomac River to the Ohio River, but it was never finished.

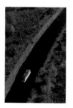 **Page 13** Horses pull the canal boat *Ben Franklin* on the Whitewater Canal in Metamora, Indiana.

 **Page 14** Adventurers, pioneers, and cargo traveled easily on the Erie Canal. The Erie opened up travel from the Great Lakes in the West to the Atlantic Ocean in the East.

 **Page 15** Lockport, New York, got its name from locks built there for the Erie Canal. The older five-step locks are on the right. Locks for larger ships (on the left) were added in the 1900s.

 **Page 16** Water in a backyard pool lifts toy boats. Pools and canals are a lot alike. Years ago, canallers (pronounced *ca-nawl-ers* to rhyme with *dollars*) swam in canals in summertime.

 **Page 17** The Corinth Canal, completed in 1893, helps ships cut across Greece from the Ionian Sea to the Aegean Sea. From the banks of the canal, boats and barges look like toys.

 **Page 18** Starting at the Soo Canals, you can travel all the way from Lake Superior to the Atlantic Ocean. But don't try to make the trip in mid-winter. These canals freeze. The canals and locks are closed until spring.

 **Page 19** Skaters love the cold weather in Ottawa, Ontario. The Rideau Canal links Ottawa and Kingston in Canada.

 **Page 20** Ships often ran aground in the sandbars off Cape Cod, Massachusetts. Many sailors lost their lives. The Cape Cod Canal takes ships away from the sandbars and into calmer waters.

 **Page 21**   The All-American Canal carries water for crops from the Hoover Dam on the Colorado River to farms in Arizona and Southern California.

 **Page 22**   A worker clears algae from an irrigation canal on Cyprus, an island in the Mediterranean Sea. Canals help people there grow potatoes, grapes, and oranges.

 **Page 23**   A dipper dredge scoops silt onto a barge, cleaning out the Panama Canal. Silt washes into all canals with rain. If left alone, silt builds up on the canal bottom. The canal becomes shallower and shallower. Ships can no longer pass through.

 **Page 24**   Have you ever slid down a water slide? It's full of water, just like a canal. It carries you over land from one place to another, too. A water slide, however, may be faster than a canal.

 **Page 25**   A worker on the Erie Canal paints the railings of Lock #8 near Rotterdam, New York. The New York State Thruway Authority maintains the Erie, now part of the New York State Barge Canal system.

 **Page 26**   The longest passenger ship ever to sail through the Panama Canal is the *Queen Elizabeth II*. She looks gigantic as she passes through the Miraflores Locks.

 **Page 27**   This section of the Erie Canal looks like a park, with its green grass and blue water. The lock in this picture is near Little Falls, New York.

 **Page 28**   Thousands of acres of farmland in California were created with the help of irrigation canals.

 **Page 29**   The Canal du Midi in France links the Atlantic Ocean to the Mediterranean Sea. It was built in the 1600s. Ben Franklin and Thomas Jefferson saw the canal while visiting France. They supported building canals in their own country, the new USA.